Samsung Galaxy S24 User guide

A comprehensive step by step manual for beginners and seniors

Frances R. Wade

Table of contents

Chapter 1: Introducing Your Galaxy S24: Unveiling The Hardware..4

Chapter 2: Making Calls and Sending Messages—Connecting with Ease in a Digital World. 11

Chapter 3: Navigating Your Phone with Confidence—Demystifying the Digital Canvas........17

Chapter 4: Connecting to the Web—Unveiling the Digital Universe...................................... 23

Chapter 5: Capturing Memories with the Camera—Your Phone's Gateway to Timeless Storytelling..29

Chapter 6: Personalizing Your Experience: Customize Your Phone to Reflect Your Unique Self... 35

Chapter 7: Increasing Productivity: Turning Your Phone into a Time-Taming Powerhouse..................41

Chapter 8: Troubleshooting and Support - Overcoming Glitches and Reaching Tech Nirvana. 47

Appendix.. 53

Chapter 1: Introducing Your Galaxy S24: Unveiling The Hardware

Welcome to the Wonderful World of Your Galaxy S24!

Congratulations for your sleek and powerful gadget! This chapter will walk you through the exciting process of meeting your new phone, getting to know its design, and comprehending the essential features that make it unique.

First impressions:

Elegant Design: As you hold your Galaxy S24, enjoy its elegant lines and high-quality materials. The smooth surface and pleasant grip provide an enjoyable usage experience.

Stunning Display: Enjoy the bright colors and crisp details of the AMOLED screen. Whether you're browsing images, viewing movies, or reading text, the display will be a visual pleasure.

Button Basics: Let's become familiar with the most important buttons around the phone:

Power Button: To switch on or off your phone, gently touch the power button on the right side.

A brief touch awakens the screen, whereas a longer push brings up the Power Menu.

level Buttons: These useful buttons, located above the Power Button, allow you to change the sound level on your phone.

 SIM Card Tray: On the left side, this little slot houses your SIM card, which links you to your cellular network.

Let us explore around:

Top Edge: This is where you'll find the headphone jack, which is ideal for connecting your preferred headphones or earbuds.

Bottom Edge This holds the charging connector, to which you will attach the provided USB-C cable to power up your phone.

Back: Take a peek at the back panel. Depending on the Galaxy S24 model, you'll get a powerful camera system with several lenses and a flash.

How to Unlock Your Samsung Adventure:

Fingerprint Sensor: Locate the specified place on the back or below the display. This is your fingerprint sensor, a safe and easy method to unlock your phone with a single touch.

Face Recognition: Some Galaxy S24 versions have face recognition technology. Look for the front-facing camera and follow the on-screen instructions to enable this additional unlocking option.

Remember:

Take your time, examine each feature, and get acquainted with the arrangement. Your Galaxy S24 is a doorway into a world of possibilities, and knowing its hardware is the first step toward maximizing its capabilities.

Turning On and Taking Your First Steps with Your Galaxy S24

Let the adventure begin!

Now that you've gotten to know the Galaxy S24's magnificent hardware, it's time to bring it to life and take your first thrilling steps into the digital world it provides. This chapter will walk you through the power-up process, introduce you to the internet world, customize your phone, and prepare you for success with a Google account.

Power Up:

- 1. Find the Power Button: As we discussed in Chapter 1, this vital button is located on the right side of your phone. Don't worry; it's not concealed! Look for the long, slim button just above the volume controls.
- 2. Hold and Release: Gently yet firmly press and hold the Power Button for a few seconds. The Samsung logo will appear on the screen, followed by an animated boot process. Relax and enjoy the visual show!
- 3. Welcome Message: Once the boot procedure is complete, you will be presented with a welcome message in your choice language. Tap "Start" to start the basic setup procedure.

Connecting with the Wireless World:

- 1. Choose Your Network: Your phone will display a list of accessible Wi-Fi networks. Choose your desired network and input your password (if applicable). This stage connects your phone to the internet, giving you access to a wealth of information and entertainment.

- 2. No WiFi? No problem! : If you don't have quick access to Wi-Fi, don't worry! You may skip this step for the time being and proceed with the setup using your mobile data. You may always reconnect to Wi-Fi later using the Settings menu.

The Wonderful World of Google
- 1. Introducing Google: Your Galaxy S24 depends heavily on Google services to provide a smooth experience. You will be requested to sign in to your current Google account or create a new one. Don't worry, setting up a Google account is free and simple!
- 2. Benefits of a Google Account: Having a Google account gives you access to a wealth of features, like access to the Play Store for app downloads, synchronizing your contacts and calendar across devices, utilizing Gmail for email communication, and using Google Maps for navigation, to name a few.
- 3. Sign In or Sign Up: If you have an existing Google account, enter your username and password. This procedure

include providing your preferred login, password, and basic information.

Make Your Homescreen Your Own:

- 1. The Gate to All Things: The homescreen is your phone's core hub, providing easy access to your favorite applications, widgets, and information. Initially, you will see pre-installed applications and simple widgets. But don't worry, it's completely customizable!
- 2. Get to Know the Icons: The colorful squares and symbols on your screen are app icons. Tap them to start the corresponding applications. Explore and familiarize yourself with these symbols, and you'll be able to navigate your homescreen with ease.
- 3. Personalized Playground: Here comes the exciting part! Hold down an app icon and drag it anywhere on the screen to rearrange it. You can also use folders to organize related programs together. To add widgets, press and hold an empty area on the screen, choose "Widgets," then pick the ones you want. Widgets provide real-time information like

weather, calendar appointments, and news headlines.

- 4. Background Magic: Customize your homescreen background to reflect your individuality. Simply press and hold an empty area, pick "Wallpaper," and choose from pre-loaded or your own photographs.

Chapter 2: Making Calls and Sending Messages—Connecting with Ease in a Digital World

In today's fast-paced world, keeping in touch with loved ones, coworkers, and business acquaintances is more crucial than ever. Fortunately, contemporary smartphones have evolved into formidable communication tools, enabling us to make calls, send text messages, and even have video conferences all from the palm of our hands. This chapter digs into the key features of making calls, sending texts, and video calling on your smartphone, allowing you to keep in contact with ease.

Basics of Telephony: A Symphony of Connections

Making and receiving calls remains the basic function of every phone, even smartphones. Let's create a seamless calling experience:

dialing in:

- 1. Open the Phone App: This app, which is often represented by a green phone symbol, acts as your entry point into the calling world.
- 2. Enter the Number: You may enter the required phone number straight into the keyboard or use your contacts list for rapid dialing.
- 3. Start the Call: Press the "Call" button to send a ring to the recipient's phone.

Receiving calls:

- 1. Incoming Call: When someone calls you, your phone will ring or vibrate, and the caller's details will appear on the screen.
- 2. Answering the Call: To answer the call, slide the "Answer" button or hit the green phone symbol.
- 3. Declining the Call: If you are unable to answer, hit the "Decline" button or the red phone symbol to direct the call to voicemail.

Contacts: Your Digital Address Book

Keeping an organized contact list is essential for effective calling. Here's how to handle your contacts like an expert:

- Adding Contacts: In your phone app, tap the "Add Contact" button and input the required information, such as name, phone number, email address, and even a photo.
- Editing Contacts: You can quickly change or update existing contact information by pressing on a contact and choosing the "Edit" option.
- Grouping Contacts: Organize your contacts into categories such as "Family," "Friends," or "Work" to facilitate navigation and rapid group calls or messaging.

Voicemail: Your Backup When You Are Unavailable

Anyone may miss a call. Fortunately, voicemail serves as a safety net, recording messages from missed calls. Here's how to manage your voicemails:

To check voicemail, use the Phone app or a carrier-specific voicemail app. To play and delete messages, listen to them, replay them if necessary, and delete them. To customize greetings, set a personalized greeting for callers.

Texting Made Easy: Expressing Yourself with Words and Emojis
Text messaging has become the preferred medium of communication for many people, providing a simple and informal way to interact. Let's learn how to write and deliver effective text messages.

- Composing a Message: Launch the "Messages" app, choose the receiver from your contacts or input their phone number directly, and begin composing your message.
- Adding Emojis: Enhance your messages with expressive emojis by pressing the emoji symbol on your keyboard. A wide collection of emojis is ready to bring individuality and fun to your texts.
- Send Multimedia: Include photographs, videos, or your location in text messages

for a more engaging communication experience.

- Group Chats: Create group chats to keep the discussion going with many contacts, which are ideal for event planning or keeping up with pals.

Video Call Convenience: Seeing is Believing

For individuals who seek face-to-face engagement, video calling offers a real-time glimpse into the lives of loved ones, regardless of distance. Here's how you can connect visually:

- Starting a Video Call: In your preferred video calling app, choose the contact you want to connect with and hit the "Video Call" button.
- Adjusting Settings: Most video calling applications let you switch between front and rear cameras, mute your microphone, or blur your backdrop for more privacy.
- Sharing Your Screen: Display your phone's screen to the other caller for

presentations, collaborative work, or just viewing films together.

Remember:
Etiquette Matters: Be cautious of call times and loudness, particularly when communicating with persons in other time zones or possibly quiet situations.

- Battery Drain: Video calls use more battery than ordinary calls, so have a charger available for long talks.
- Data Usage: Video calls need data, so ensure you have a suitable data plan or are connected to Wi-Fi for flawless video.

Chapter 3: Navigating Your Phone with Confidence—Demystifying the Digital Canvas

Your phone, a sleek slab in your hand, contains more than just applications and games; it is a gateway to knowledge, connection, and limitless possibilities. However, in order to reach its full potential, it must first understand the language it speaks: touch movements. In this chapter, we'll take a voyage through your phone's UI, decoding the cryptic language of swipes, taps, and holds to convert you into a competent digital navigator.

- Touch Gestures, the Invisible Ink of Interaction
- Consider your fingers to be invisible ink brushes that paint orders and requests on the phone's glass canvas. Mastering these basic motions allows you to interact with your device with the elegance of an experienced artist:

- The Mighty Tap: A single tap, similar to a polite knock, launches an app, opens a file, or activates a button. Double press to zoom in, an intriguing peak into the digital world, or triple touch for immediate action, a power play for easy access.
- The Art of Swiping: Consider swiping as skimming the surface of digital ink. A vertical swipe, similar to flipping the pages of a book, may be used to scroll up and down web pages and lists. Use a horizontal swipe to navigate between tabs or photographs, going through the chapters of your digital life. Diagonal swipes, secret handshakes for hidden functions, revealing hidden menus, or activating special features in certain programs.
- Hold and Behold: A touch and hold, a lingering caress, selects text, opens the context menu for more investigation, or previews a picture, providing a tantalizing glance before delving in. Swipe and hold, a gentle guidance, rearranges your home screen by dragging and dropping app icons, transfers files

between digital folders, and modifies text selection like sculpting digital clay.

Home Screen: Your Personal Portal

Consider the home screen to be your digital living room, where you may express your wants and requirements. Here's how to make it an oasis of ordered efficiency:

- App Placement: Drag and drop icons, much like rearranging furniture, to create a layout that works with your natural interaction. To keep your digital pantry clutter-free, organize comparable programs into folders, which are neatly stacked baskets. Use folders inside folders and hidden drawers for less regular visitors to retain accessibility without visual overload.
- Widgets: Windows to Information: Think of widgets as windows onto various parts of your digital life. Add weather predictions for a look at the sky, or news headlines for an update on the globe. Long-press and resize them to meet your information demands, making your home screen seem like a lovely landscape.

Interactive widgets, like mini-apps, may play music or send messages with a single swipe, transforming your home screen into a lively marketplace of rapid activities.

The Notification Panel, Your Digital Town Crier The notification display serves as a constant herald, informing you of the digital world's murmurs and yells. Swipe down from the top, as if opening a window, to see incoming calls, texts, app notifications, and system updates. Tap on a notice, such as a town crier's call, to access the appropriate app or learn more about the information. To clean your screen and recover concentration, swipe away individual alerts as if you were dusting the windowsill. Use the "Clear All" button, a dramatic declaration of closure, to wipe the slate clear and start again.

Customization is Important: Try out alternative home screen layouts, widget locations, and notification settings. Explore accessibility features like as voice control, bigger fonts, and high contrast settings to build a phone that meets your specific requirements and preferences. Remember that your phone is an extension of yourself; customize it to sing your tune!

Stay updated: Software updates are more than simply digital housekeeping; they may provide new features, resolve bugs, and boost performance. Accept them as improvements to your digital companion, ensuring that your phone handles the ever-changing digital world with elegance and simplicity.

By learning five fundamental abilities, you can change your phone from a perplexing enigma to a trusted companion. Each touch, swipe, and hold initiates a dialog, with a whispered request receiving an instant answer. With confidence at your fingertips, you set out on a trip of limitless possibilities, navigating the digital world with the ease of a seasoned explorer, your phone serving as your trusted compass.

Remember, the phone is just a tool. The ultimate magic is in how you utilize it to connect, create, and discover. So, courageous navigator, choose your own route over the wide and fascinating digital ocean!

Chapter 4: Connecting to the Web—Unveiling the Digital Universe

With a touch on your phone's screen, you enter the web, a vast ocean of knowledge, social connections, and limitless possibilities. This chapter provides you with the necessary skills to traverse the wide digital environment, from riding the waves of search engines to anchoring yourself in the dynamic archipelago of social media.

Browsing the Internet: Choosing Your Path across the Digital Sea

Consider your phone to be a sleek ship ready to cruise over the vast internet sea. Let us hoist the sails of the web browser app and begin on a journey of discovery:

- Exploring the web: Start your chosen browser app, the captain's map of the digital seas. Tap on familiar landmarks - websites you've been to previously - or explore new territory by typing a web address into the search field.

- Looking for information: Consider the search box to be a compass directing you through the information tempest. Enter your inquiry, a whispered quest for information, and watch as the search engine returns a net of possible answers. Examine the findings, comparing and contrasting them like a seasoned pirate combing through treasure maps.
- Opening websites: Each website is a distinct island in the digital archipelago, brimming with content, tools, and experiences. Tap on a search result to put your anchor on the desired website, walking into its digital beaches and immersing yourself in its content.

Emailing Made Simple: Establishing Communication in the Digital Sea

Email, the digital carrier pigeon, enables you to send and receive messages from anywhere on the internet. Here's how to use this crucial communication tool:

- Sending an Email: Launch your built-in email software and choose the "Compose" button. As with a blank scroll, begin by inputting the recipient's address in the "To" column, determining who your message will reach over the digital waves. Compose your message in the email body, carefully weaving your words together, and attach photographs, documents, or links as appropriate. Finally, hit "Send" to start your message's trip.

- Receiving and Managing Emails: Check your inbox, which is the port where new communications arrive. Open emails to read the contents and respond or forward them as required. Use folders and labels to arrange your email like a geographer carefully chronicling the digital environment.

- Stay Connected and Organized: Remember that email etiquette counts. Keep your communications brief and professional, and avoid sharing important information over unprotected connections. With regular use and management, email may become a reliable digital lifeline, linking you with loved ones, coworkers, and opportunities all across the world.

Staying Social: Bridging the Social Media Islands

From news updates to kitten videos, social media platforms are thriving sources of connection and community. Let's visit these colorful islands and develop bridges with our friends and family.

- Identifying Your Favorite Platforms: Different platforms appeal to various interests. Explore popular alternatives such as Facebook, Instagram, Twitter, and TikTok, each of which provides unique ways to share and interact. Choose the platforms that speak to your needs and hobbies, and discover your digital tribe among the massive online population.
- Creating Your Profile: Consider your profile to be your digital homestead, a place where you may express your personality and hobbies. Create an engaging profile, share pictures and videos, and organize your page to convey your own unique narrative.

- Connecting and Engaging: Stay up to speed on the lives of friends and family by following them, similar to sending smoke signals over digital plains. Share articles, comments, and experiences, such as giving presents to other travelers, to start discussions and make significant relationships.

Remember:
- Safety First: Be cautious about what you disclose online, and only connect with individuals you trust. Use privacy settings to manage who may view your information, and use strong passwords to safeguard your accounts.
- Digital balance: While social media may be beneficial, too much screen time can be harmful. Take pauses, emphasize real-world connections, and make sure your digital life enhances, not consumes, your offline life.
- Explore and adapt: Social media platforms are always evolving. Stay up to date on new features, investigate their potential, and adjust your use to reflect the evolving digital scene.

By acquiring these fundamental abilities, you may turn your phone from a mere communication tool into a gateway to a large and lively digital world. You become an experienced navigator, able to plan your way over the internet's vast oceans, convey messages across digital waves, and construct bridges of connection on the buzzing islands of social media.

Chapter 5: Capturing Memories with the Camera—Your Phone's Gateway to Timeless Storytelling

The camera is nestled inside the elegant frame of your smartphone, serving as a conduit to narrative magic. It's a window into the vivid fabric of life, with the ability to capture ephemeral moments and turn them into treasured memories. This chapter, your visual alchemy guide, teaches you how to go beyond point-and-shoot photography and turn your phone into a digital time capsule filled with rich storylines.

Uncovering the Camera's Secrets: Demystifying the Buttons and Sliders

Your phone's camera software may seem to be a confusing menu of buttons and symbols, but do not worry, wannabe storytellers! Let's reveal its secrets and give you the tools to release your inner artist:

- Modes: Each mode represents a brush stroke on your digital canvas. Auto, for simple daily captures, lets you point and shoot with simplicity. Portrait mode creates a gentle blur around your subject, similar to what a professional lens would produce. Night mode adds breathtaking detail to even the darkest situations, highlighting the wonder of moonlight. Explore each mode like a painter, experimenting with various colors until you discover the one that best fits your tale.
- Composition Is King: Consider your screen to be a canvas, with the rule of thirds serving as a guideline. For dynamic compositions, place your subject off-center and use leading lines like as roads or fences to drive the viewer's attention into the core of your tale. Don't be hesitant to defy the rules; a centered topic or an unusual viewpoint may lend a touch of creative flair.
- Light, the stage director: Light, the artist's paintbrush, dances over your sceneries. Learn to use its power like a director establishing the mood: revel in

the warm glow of the golden hour for sun-kissed pictures, embrace backlighting for dramatic shadows, or use reflections in puddles and windows to create depth and curiosity. Remember that light may convert an everyday landscape into a stunning masterpiece.

- Focus Pulls You In: Tap on your subject, the scene's star, to alter the focus for sharp clarity. In low-light situations, tap and hold to engage a focus lock, which keeps your tale stable even in the shadows.

Painting with Pixels: From Everyday Snapshots to Stunning Images

Go beyond the banal and convert your photographs into compelling narratives:

- Become Intimate: Do not be frightened to zoom in! Close-ups highlight the exquisite features of a flower, the gleam in someone's eye, or the aged texture of a leaf, bringing your photographs to life and engaging the spectator into the tale.
- Embrace Different Perspectives: Forget eye-level vision! Climb a hill for a

breathtaking view, hunch low for a dramatic viewpoint, or experiment with high angles for a new twist. Changing your viewpoint provides visual interest and keeps your audience interested.

- Let Color Tell the Story: Consider the power of color. Vibrant colors exude vitality, but subdued tones induce tranquility. Choose a dominating color palette or experiment with contrasting tones to create a mood and establish the tone for your visual story.
- Catch the Unexpected: Don't simply photograph the obvious. Seek for quirky elements, brief moments, and genuine emotions that capture the soul of a situation. These surprising jewels elevate your picture portfolio.

From Captured Frames to Moving Stories: Learning the Art of Video Storytelling

Turn your phone into a mini-film studio with these video-making tips:

- Stability is Important: Shaky film may transform a masterpiece into a hassle.

Hold your phone stable or use a tripod to get smooth, professional-looking photos. Pan gently and avoid abrupt motions to ensure your viewers can enjoy the visual feast you've produced.

- Sound matters: Do not underestimate the power of sounds. Record in a calm setting for clearer capture, and consider using an external microphone for better quality. Allow the sounds of laughing, rains, or busy city streets to add another level of immersion to your narrative.
- Editing: The Last Brushstroke: Most phones provide rudimentary editing features. Trim down unneeded sections, add music or vocal narration, and use transitions to connect your video into a coherent story. Consider it the finishing brushstrokes in refining your visual masterpiece.
- Embrace Diverse Viewpoints: Don't be limited to eye-level photos! Get low for dramatic effect, high for a bird's-eye perspective, or even a Dutch angle for a bit of cinematic flare. Variety provides visual appeal and keeps your audience interested as your tale unfolds.

Remember:
Respect the lens: When taking images or videos, remember to respect your privacy and get authorization. Always get permission before photographing someone, particularly in delicate circumstances. Remember that although your camera may convey stories, you must also be a responsible narrator.

Chapter 6: Personalizing Your Experience: Customize Your Phone to Reflect Your Unique Self

Your phone is more than just a technology; it's a reflection of your personality and a gateway to your digital world. This chapter teaches you how to change it from a generic device into a personalized sanctuary that meets your needs, preferences, and accessibility requirements. In this section, we'll look at how to personalize your phone so that it not only functions for you but also seems like a treasured expression of your distinct personality.

Display Settings: A Canvas for Comfort and Clarity.
Consider your phone's display to be a canvas, and the settings your palette. We'll create a setting of visual comfort and clarity.

- Brightness and Contrast: Change the brightness to match your surroundings, reducing it for comfortable nights and turning it up for sunny days. Experiment with contrast to achieve the ideal balance between sharp text and bright colors.

- Font Size and Style: Do not squint! Increase the font size for easier reading, or choose a style that matches your personality. You may choose between a whimsical handwritten font and a sleek serif typeface.
- Color Themes: Anyone interested in dark mode? Dive into the world of color themes, choosing a traditional light theme or embracing the sleekness of dark mode to alleviate eye strain in low-light situations. Add bold accent colors to express your particular taste.
- Night Light: Protect your eyes from the blue light generated by your device before sleep. Use the night light option to provide a warmer, sleep-inducing glow.

Accessibility Features: Opening the Door to Universal Usability

Technology should be available to everybody. Fortunately, your phone is packed with a variety of capabilities to cater to unique needs:

- Vision Settings: Improve your visual experience with options like as text magnification, color modifications, and even a voice reader that narrates on-screen text. This opens up a world of knowledge and engagement for those with vision impairments.
- Listening and Audio: Use Bluetooth hearing aids or alter audio settings such as volume and balance to improve sound quality for those who have hearing problems. Closed captioning on videos and real-time transcription of phone conversations help to overcome the communication gap.
- Motor skills and dexterity: Those with limited touch dexterity may use AssistiveTouch to access a virtual home button. Voice control enables you to operate your phone and do things hands-free, enabling those with motor skill limitations.

Remember: Everyone deserves access to technology. Explore your phone's accessibility features and customize them to meet your requirements. Open the doors to a world of knowledge, connection, and freedom for yourself or someone you care about.

Security and Privacy: Create a Digital Fortress

Your phone contains a treasure mine of personal information. Learn to protect your digital empire with care.

- Strong Passwords: Avoid "123456"! Make strong, unique passwords for each app and account. Consider using a password manager to make things simpler.
- Biometric Authentication: Fingerprint sensors and face recognition provide simple and safe methods for unlocking your phone. Remember, your face and fingerprints, not just your phone, need protection.
- Software Updates: Remain watchful! Install software updates as soon as possible to fix security vulnerabilities and safeguard your phone from the newest threats.
- App Permissions: Become the gatekeeper! Monitor and alter app permissions carefully, allowing access

only to features required for proper operation. Be aware of applications that require unneeded rights, such as your location or contacts.

- Antivirus and Anti-Malware: Consider installing reputed antivirus and anti-malware software to provide an additional layer of security. Remember that prevention is always preferable than cure in the digital domain.

Remember: Security and privacy are not optional; they are essential. Be proactive in protecting your data, be aware of your online footprint, and do not hesitate to seek assistance if you see any questionable behavior.

Personalization is key. This chapter provides you with the tools you need to customize your phone's settings, accessibility features, and security measures to meet your specific requirements and preferences. Embrace experimentation, figure out what works best for you, and remember that your phone is a blank canvas ready to be customized into a representation of your digital self. Take pleasure in creating your own refuge of comfort, efficiency, and security in an ever-changing digital environment.

Chapter 7: Increasing Productivity: Turning Your Phone into a Time-Taming Powerhouse

Consider your phone not just a source of information and connection, but also a powerful weapon in your struggle against the terrible procrastination monster. This chapter will provide you with the skills and tactics you need to turn your phone from a digital distraction to a productivity powerhouse, allowing you to conquer your to-do list and regain control of your time.

Calendar and reminders: Your Time Management Arsenal

Consider your phone's calendar and reminders to be your own time-traveling generals, charting your route and making sure you never miss a beat.

- Mastering the Calendar: Plan appointments, deadlines, and crucial activities with painstaking accuracy. Use several calendar views (daily, weekly, or monthly) to see your schedule and detect possible time conflicts. Color-code categories for easier identification (blue for work, green for personal, etc.) and create repeating events for chores such as weekly exercises or monthly bill payments.

- A Gentle Nudge of Reminders: Do not let crucial work fall through the gaps! Set up reminders for deadlines, errands, and even medicine regimes. Customize the alert tone and timing to ensure that they capture your attention without becoming bothersome alerts. Integrate reminders with your location so that they appear when you arrive at specified locations, such as a grocery shop.
- Mastering Multitasking: Do not attempt to manage a dozen activities at once! Use your calendar and reminders to set up concentrated work periods for certain projects. Avoid distractions during these times and reward yourself for finishing tasks on schedule. Remember that quality work outweighs quantity, and small bursts of concentrated effort may

outperform hours of dispersed concentration.

Notes and To-Do Lists: Managing the Chaos in Your Head

Your mind is a frenzy of thoughts, chores, and shopping lists. Use your phone's notes and to-do applications as a digital brain dump, catching the chaos and changing it into a controllable system:

- Note-taking Nirvana: Get rid of bits of paper and disorganized notebooks. Use note-taking applications to record ephemeral thoughts, brainstorming sessions, and meeting minutes. Organize your notes into categories and tags to make them more searchable and accessible. Experiment with several note-taking forms, such as text, voice recordings, and even hand-drawn drawings, to discover the one that works best for you.
- The magic of to-do lists: Divide major projects into smaller, more manageable chores and arrange them with a comprehensive to-do list software.

Prioritize projects, set deadlines, and mark them off as you do them, letting the gratifying progress bar fill up with a feeling of success. Celebrate achieving milestones and reward yourself for keeping on track.

- Embrace the Synergy: Combine your notes and task lists. Link pertinent notes to individual tasks, include notes inside list items for further details, and use cross-referencing to keep your information linked and accessible.

The Power of Google Assistant: A Hands-Free Productivity Genie

Google Assistant, your ubiquitous digital companion, is waiting on your phone, ready to answer questions, execute chores, and optimize your life with the power of voice commands:

- Hands-free Hero: Forget the keyboard and experience hands-free control. Set alarms, send messages, and play music with simple voice commands. While cooking, you may ask Assistant to convert temperatures, set timers, or even add products to your shopping list. During a run, receive real-time instructions or adjust your music without fiddling with your phone.

- Information at your fingertips: Need rapid answers? You may ask Assistant anything, including weather updates, sports scores, movie showtimes, and challenging trivia questions. Get news updates, monitor traffic conditions, and translate languages without leaving your present app or work.
- Automation is essential: Create unique routines to automate daily chores. Wake up to your favorite music and weather report, control your smart home gadgets, or receive traffic updates on your commute - all with easy voice commands. Allow Assistant to handle the routine, freeing up your brain resources for more challenging activities.

Remember:
- Technology Is A Tool: Your phone is a great productivity tool, but it's still just that. Don't get addicted to frequent alerts and digital diversions. Take pauses, unplug when required, and strike a

healthy balance between digital productivity and real-world activities.

- Try and Customize: Don't be scared to try various applications and settings to see what works best for you. Create a system that matches your own workflow and organizational approach.
- Celebrate Small Wins. Monitor your progress, recognize your accomplishments, and reward yourself for continuing on track. Positive reinforcement promotes positive behaviors and keeps you motivated on your path to productivity mastery.

Chapter 8: Troubleshooting and Support - Overcoming Glitches and Reaching Tech Nirvana

Even the most polished smartphone may sometimes slip. Don't allow a frozen screen or slow performance ruin your internet experience! This chapter will provide you with the information and tools you need to successfully resolve common problems and maintain your Samsung phone running at optimal performance.

Common Issues and Solutions: A Tech-Savvy Toolbox

Think of your phone like a reliable automobile, and these troubleshooting ideas as your mechanic's toolkit:

- Battery Drain: A fast-draining battery might create worry. Check for background programs that are wasting power. Force-quit unneeded programs, adjust screen brightness, and consider using battery-saving mode for prolonged use. Remember that location services and Bluetooth may be battery hogs; turn them off when not in use.

- Slow Performance: A slow phone might be a productivity killer. Restart your device often to delete temporary files and free up memory. To guarantee optimal performance, update your applications as well as the OS on your phone. Consider removing any unnecessary programs that may be consuming resources.
- Connectivity Problems: Lost Wi-Fi or cellular data is like trekking through a digital wilderness. Check your network settings and restart your router or modem. To refresh connections, enable and deactivate airplane mode.
- App Crashes: Unexpected app crashes might disturb your workflow. Force-quit the app, restart your phone, and check that both the app and your phone's OS are up to current. If the crashes continue, remove and reinstall the program. Consider looking through web complaints for known app faults and possible solutions.

- Frozen Screen: This digital nightmare will send chills down your spine. Do not panic! To force a restart, press and hold the power and volume down keys simultaneously. If the screen remains frozen, please contact Samsung support for more help.

Remember: Before you begin any extensive troubleshooting, back up your vital data to the cloud or an external storage device. It is better to be cautious than sorry!

Getting Help and Resources: If in Doubt, Reach Out

Even the greatest toolset may benefit from a helping hand. Don't hesitate to take use of the abundance of resources available:

- Samsung Support: The first line of defense. The official Samsung support website and app provide detailed troubleshooting manuals, FAQs, and live chat help to handle your unique needs. They also provide device-specific information and repair choices.

- On-line Communities: Join the lively crowds of tech aficionados! Samsung phone forums and internet groups include a wealth of useful information and advice. Share your problem, look through previous discussions for answers, or seek advice from other individuals.
- Social media: Social media isn't just for cat videos! Many technological businesses, like Samsung, provide direct customer service via platforms such as Twitter and Facebook. Connect with a representative and obtain specialized support by tweeting, messaging, or posting about your concern.

Proactive Maintenance: Prevention Is Key

Remember that even the smoothest ride might benefit from regular checkups. Here are some suggestions to reduce future issues:

-
- Software Updates: Become an update expert! Install software updates as soon as possible to take advantage of bug fixes, performance improvements, and

increased security. Enable auto-updates for maximum convenience.

- App Management: On a regular basis, review your applications and remove those that are no longer in use. Keep an eye on the permissions provided to programs and only download trustworthy apps from reliable sources.
- Battery Care: Treat your battery like queen! Avoid excessive heat and overcharging. To extend the life of your battery, consider purchasing a high-quality charger and cord.
- Backup Data: Do not risk losing valuable memories! Backup your vital data on a regular basis to the cloud or an external storage device. Peace of mind is ensured.

Remember: With a little know-how and the correct resources, you can confidently address the majority of frequent phone difficulties. Don't be hesitant to ask for assistance, and remember that proactive maintenance is your secret weapon for keeping your Samsung phone functioning like new.

Appendix.

A glossary of terms:

- AMOLED: (Active-Matrix Organic Light-Emitting Diode). The display technology noted for its brilliant colors, deep blacks, and strong contrast. Android: The operating system powering most smartphones, including Samsung's Galaxy range.
- APEX (Application Execution Environment) manages and separates programs on Android devices to improve security and performance. APK (Android Package Kit) is the file format for distributing and installing Android apps.
- App: An application is a software program intended to perform certain activities on a mobile device.
- Backlight refers to the light source behind an LCD panel that illuminates the pixels. Bluetooth is a wireless technology used for short-range data transmission.
- CPU (Central Processing Unit): Your phone's brain, which processes information and commands.

- Data: Digital information such as photos, videos, documents, and music.
- Firmware: Low-level software that controls your phone's hardware.
- GB (Gigabyte): A storage capacity unit equal to 1 billion bytes.
- GPS (Global Positioning System): A satellite-based system for navigating your location.
- GPU (Graphics Processing Unit): Processes graphics and visuals to ensure smooth performance in games and videos.
- OS (Operating System): The software that handles your phone's hardware and software resources, including the interface with which you interact.
- RAM (Random Access Memory): Temporary storage utilized by your phone to store current applications and data.
- ROM (Read-Only Memory): Permanent storage for the operating system and other critical phone operations.
- SIM card (Subscriber Identity Module): A tiny chip that identifies your phone via a mobile network.

- Software: The collection of instructions that informs your phone what to do, including applications and the operating system.
- USB (Universal Serial Bus) is a standard for connecting devices and exchanging data.
- Wi-Fi: A wireless technology for connecting to the internet via a local network.

Index:

- Accessibility Features (Chapter 6)
- Application crashes (Chapter 8).
- Application management (Chapter 8)
- Battery Care (Chapter 8).
- Bluetooth (see Chapter 8, Glossary)
- Brightness Settings (Chapter 6)
- Calendar and Reminders (Chapter 7)
- Camera Basics (Chapter 5).
- Color Themes (Chapter 6)
- Connectivity Issues (Chapter 8)
- Display Settings (Chapter 6).
- Font sizes and styles (Chapter 6)
- Getting Help and Resources (Chapter 8)
- Google Assistant (Chapter7)
- Index (Appendix).
- Light effect (Chapter 5).
- Location Settings (Chapter 6)
- Nightlight (Chapter 6).
- Notes and task lists (Chapter 7)
- Personalization (Chapter Six)
- Capturing amazing photos (Chapter 5)
- Chapters 5 and 8 cover portrait mode and proactive maintenance.
- Security and Privacy (Chapter 6).
- Slow performance (Chapter 8).
- Software Updates (Chapter 8)

- Troubleshooting frequent difficulties (Chapter 8).
- Video, recording remarkable (Chapter 5).
- Wi-Fi (see Chapter 8, Glossary)

www.ingramcontent.com/pod-product-compliance
Lightning Source LLC
LaVergne TN
LVHW051620050326

832903LV00033B/4588